Caring for the Earth

Let's Reuse!

by Sara E. Nelson

Consulting Editor: Gail Saunders-Smith, PhD

Consultant: Kate M. Krebs
Executive Director, National Recycling Coalition, Inc.

Capstone press®
Mankato, Minnesota

Pebble Books are published by Capstone Press,
151 Good Counsel Drive, P.O. Box 669, Mankato, Minnesota 56002.
www.capstonepress.com

1 2 3 4 5 6 11 10 09 08 07 06

Library of Congress Cataloging-in-Publication Data
Nelson, Sara Elizabeth.
Let's reuse! / Sara E. Nelson.
p. cm.—(Pebble books. Caring for the earth)
Summary: "Simple text and photographs describe easy ways to reuse items
and why it is important to do so"—Provided by publisher.
Includes bibliographical references and index.
ISBN-13: 978-0-7368-6325-4 (hardcover)
ISBN-10: 0-7368-6325-7 (hardcover)
1. Waste minimization—Juvenile literature. 2. Conservation of natural
resources—Juvenile literature. I. Title. II. Series.
TD793.9.N46 2007
363.72'82—dc22   2006006392

Note to Parents and Teachers

The Caring for the Earth set supports national science standards
related to conservation and environmental change. This book
describes and illustrates ways children can reuse common items.
The images support early readers in understanding the text. The
repetition of words and phrases helps early readers learn new
words. This book also introduces early readers to subject-specific
vocabulary words, which are defined in the Glossary section.
Early readers may need assistance to read some words and to
use the Table of Contents, Glossary, Read More, Internet Sites,
and Index sections of the book.

Table of Contents

Too Much Garbage!

Joe throws away garbage every day. Where does it go?

Some garbage goes
to landfills.
Our landfills
are filling up quickly.

Ways to Reuse

Many items people use don't have to become garbage. Beth washes a plastic tub. Then it can be reused.

Now the tub
holds crayons.
Yogurt cups make
good paint cups.

Max reuses a milk carton to pot a plant.

Kim's family buys items they can use many times. Kim uses her lunch box and water bottle again and again.

You can share
your ideas for reusing.
How would you reuse
these items?

Caring for the Earth

Maria gives items
to other people
so they can reuse them.
Then Maria has
less garbage.

Reusing items
makes less garbage.
Less garbage keeps
the Earth healthy.

Glossary

garbage—items people throw away because they don't need or use them anymore

landfill—an area of land where garbage is placed and then buried

plastic—a material that is made into different shapes; plastic has many uses.

reuse—to use items again so they don't need to be thrown away

Read More

Bedford, Deborah Jackson. *Garbage Disposal.* Action for the Environment. North Mankato, Minn.: Smart Apple Media, 2005.

Ganeri, Anita. *Something Old, Something New: Recycling.* Chicago: Heinemann, 2005.

Internet Sites

FactHound offers a safe, fun way to find Internet sites related to this book. All of the sites on FactHound have been researched by our staff.

Here's how:

1. Visit *www.facthound.com*
2. Choose your grade level.
3. Type in this book ID **0736863257** for age-appropriate sites. You may also browse subjects by clicking on letters, or by clicking on pictures and words.
4. Click on the **Fetch It** button.

FactHound will fetch the best sites for you!

Index

Earth, 21

garbage, 5, 7,
    9, 19, 21

giving, 19

healthy, 21

ideas, 17

landfills, 7

lunch box, 15

milk carton, 13

plastic tub, 9, 11

washing, 9

water bottle, 15

Word Count: 120
Grade: 1
Early-Intervention Level: 15

Editorial Credits
Mari Schuh, editor; Juliette Peters, designer; Wanda Winch, photo researcher;
    Scott Thoms, photo editor

Photo Credits
Capstone Press/Karon Dubke, cover, 1, 4, 8, 10, 12, 14, 16 (both), 18
Getty Images Inc./The Image Bank/Britt Erlanson, 20
SuperStock Inc./SuperStock, 6

Capstone Press thanks Jean Lundquist, waste management specialist in Blue Earth
County's Environmental Services Department in Mankato, Minnesota, for her
helpful assistance with this book.